"Podcastnomics should quickly become the bible for podcasting."
— Kerry Lutz, Founder of the Financial Survival Network

PODCASTNOMICS

The Book Of Podcasting...

To Make You Millions

By Naresh Vissa

FOREWORD BY:

Jason Hartman
Founder & CEO
The Hartman Media Company

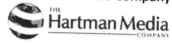

AFTERWORD BY:

Rob Walch
Vice President of Podcaster Relations
Libsyn

Praise for Podcastnomics

"*Podcastnomics* fires on all cylinders. I've been waiting for the definitive podcast guide to hand my new clients for years. This is now a manual for my engineers and required reading for my new clients... a home run for modern podcasters and a staple on the studio bookshelf."

—Corey Coates, Co-owner of Podfly Productions

"*Podcastnomics* should quickly become the bible for podcasting. Everything one needs to become a successful podcaster is contained herein. I could have saved much time and effort in building the Financial Survival Network if *Podcastnomics* was available three years ago."

—Kerry Lutz, Founder of the Financial Survival Network

"There are many good reasons on why you should podcast. This book has covered those reasons well."

—Rob Walch, VP of Podcaster Relations at Libsyn

"As an avid traveler who has visited 71 countries, I love the freedom to record my shows from anywhere in the world. Naresh provides details in this book so you can too."

—Jason Hartman, Founder & CEO of The Hartman Media Company

"Podcasting is the ultimate engagement mechanism in our digital world because people of all walks of life can create and establish their own brand and their own community... not to mention, you can sell a LOT of stuff without trying very hard at all, and Naresh walks you through it perfectly in this book!"

—Jason Drohn, Marketing Expert & Author

Naresh Vissa
PODCASTNOMICS: The Book Of Podcasting... To Make You Millions

ISBN-13: 978-0692268889 (Krish Publishing)
ISBN-10: 069226888X

CONTENTS

DEDICATION

To all of my past and current media clients... some of you gave me a chance to learn on the fly as a college student... others believed enough to invest in my visions.

ABOUT THE AUTHOR

Naresh Vissa is a media, marketing and publishing entrepreneur, specializing in product launches and marketing strategy and execution.

Vissa started his media career as an editor at his high school newspaper. He went on to host, report and produce various print, TV, terrestrial radio shows and podcasts while studying full-time during his undergraduate and graduate educations. He has helped his clients make millions of dollars through podcasting.

Born and raised in Houston, Texas, Vissa graduated Magna Cum Laude from Syracuse University's Honors Program with degrees in broadcast journalism, finance and accounting. He earned a Master's Degree in Management Studies from Duke University's Fuqua School of Business.

Vissa has been featured on USA Today, Yahoo!, Bloomberg, MSNBC, Huffington Post, Business Week, MSN Money, Business Insider, India Today, Hindustan Times and other domestic and international media outlets.

Subscribe to Naresh Vissa's free *Podcastnomics* mailing list at www.podcastnomics.com.

If you have any questions about podcasting, contact Naresh Vissa at naresh dot vissa at gmail.com.

PODCASTNOMICS

The Book Of Podcasting... To Make You Millions

FOREWORD

By Jason Hartman, Founder & CEO of The Hartman Media Company

Podcasting has improved my life and business in so many ways. I grew up with very limited resources and opportunities, so I was highly motivated to improve my lot in life at a very young age. This drive helped me create early and continued success throughout my career. I started in real estate part-time while attending college at the ripe old age of 19. Just a few years later, at age 24, I was one of the top realtors in the world. I used – what would later be known as personal branding by advertising – my services everywhere I could: newspapers, magazines, TV, radio shows and, most importantly, something called "farming." This is a technique used by real estate people where they focus on a small geographical area and become, as the title of my first book says, "The Brand of Choice." Farming and podcasting are all about trust and community. More on this later.

But at the turn of the millennium, advertising was changing rapidly. There was a time when one of my companies was spending around $250,000 per year on radio advertising. The returns were okay, but the quality of these cold leads was not ideal since they didn't know us and didn't understand what we did.

I also had my own radio show in Los Angeles. That was okay, but not great, so I focused on presenting live seminars, which had excellent returns/conversion but required me to be there in person so scalability and duplication was limited. I love public speaking and people say I'm very good at it, but it can be exhausting after several speaking engagements each month.

In 2007, I created *The Creating Wealth* podcast to promote my real estate investment business, and the podcast quickly became the number one way to build a community of loyal fans... some would even say groupies and a cult-like following... think Harley-Davidson and Apple on a smaller scale.

I now run a network including 20 different podcasts with over 1,200 episodes and listeners in 164 countries. The shows cover various niches within business, personal finance, preparedness, politics, health, asset protection, travel, longevity, marketing and more. Visit www.HartmanMedia.com to see all the current titles.

As an avid traveler who has visited 71 countries so far, I love the freedom to record my shows from anywhere in the world. Naresh will provide the details in this book so you can too. I've built up an audience that listens to me, even when I'm not working. That's even better than passive income – it's "passive influence."

Now, I spend very little time or money on advertising. Instead, my podcasts bring in high quality, highly trusted and highly educated leads to my businesses.

The great thing about podcasting is that the business you get is business that finds you. The traffic is organic. People actually want to listen to you. It's the highest form of Seth Godin's "Permission Marketing." They find you, self-select and enthusiastically opt-in. They come prequalified and already versed in our philosophies, ready to purchase products and services. They are already extremely well educated and that is the best kind of customer to have.

I can attribute more than $10 million in revenue (not sales, but actual INCOME) through my podcasts. It's the way we get most of our business.

Podcasting has afforded me the opportunity to talk to big-name celebrity thought-leaders like Steve Forbes and so many others at length. I've had dozens of *New York Times* best-selling authors like Jack Canfield, two mainstream presidential candidates and almost got a third, Ron Paul, who I plan to invite again, on my shows. I've gained access to people who would have never been available to me without being a member of the media, and this is available to you too.

As my show guest and friend, James Altucher, depicts in the title of his excellent book, "Choose Yourself": you don't have to be vetted by some radio or television executive, a literary agent or a publisher. You have direct access to the free market.

If you have something to say that you think is valuable, start a podcast. It's almost free. You can get your message out to the world, whether it's a business, a hobby, a political philosophy or a good charitable cause. Never before in history have we had this opportunity.

Much success and happy podcasting!

Jason Hartman
Founder & CEO of The Hartman Media Company

INTRODUCTION

Podcast (noun) – a program (as of music or talk) made available in digital format for automatic download over the Internet
- Merriam-Webster Dictionary

Podcasting is an incredibly niche area of media production, online marketing and sales strategy. Talk to a marketing director at any company, and it's likely they'll know little to nothing about podcasting and its benefits in improving a firm's brand, publicity, awareness, goodwill and overall sales.

But just like any project in the business world, execution is key. That's what this book is about... how YOU can start a podcast, with very little investment, and make money through it.

My Experience With Podcasting

In 2008, I started out in terrestrial radio while attending college. I worked at the only dedicated business talk radio station in Houston, called The BizRadio Network. I learned all about media production: sales, marketing, audio editing, guest booking, rundowns, and more. The internship was extremely worthwhile and even put a good chunk of change in my pocket.

Despite the experience, I quickly realized terrestrial radio was dying. The station was bleeding for money. Advertising revenue was poor. The overhead to produce the shows was insane. It wasn't a sustainable business model.

After my term ended, the station owners offered me a part-time job to continue working while attending school at Syracuse University, where I was a broadcast journalism, finance and accounting triple major. I accepted without hesitation. The decision ended up paving an entrepreneurial path that I will never regret.

Over the past seven years, I've produced, managed and hosted more than 25 terrestrial radio shows and podcasts. Now, I fill in as host on some podcasts and am working on starting my own.

I've reported for print, radio, TV and online media. I have print, broadcasting, editorial and production experience. I launched a new online radio and podcasting division for one of the largest private and independent financial publishers in the world. It produces some of the highest-rated business podcasts on iTunes.

I've started podcasts for various businesses. Some succeeded, and some failed.

This book lays out, in detail, what I've learned in the process.

Podcastnomics

Before we get to the meat, I want to expound on the subtitle of this book: "The Book Of Podcasting... To Make You Millions." To clarify, I personally have not made millions of dollars from podcasting, but I've helped my clients do it. In fact, one of my clients has made more than $10 million (as discussed in the foreword). I've made a good living from this niche expertise... just not millions of dollars.

Chapter 1
THE DEATH OF RADIO

N obody's listening to radio anymore. By radio, I mean the same radio our parents listened to: AM/FM terrestrial radio. We used to listen to this too, albeit 10-15 years ago.

There are too many <u>digital devices that take away from drive time listening</u>: audiobooks, iPods with music and podcasts, Bluetooth on Smartphones, etc.

In 2010, Edison Research found that the amount of time millennials spend listening to radio per day has fallen by nearly 50% during the first decade of the millennium, from two hours and 43 minutes a day to an hour and a half. Terrestrial radio is now the third most listened to medium behind TV and the Internet. It used to be first.

In 2013, the NPD Group reported that the numbers for terrestrial radio got worse. Smartphones have become ubiquitous, so streaming apps like Pandora, iTunes and Spotify stole more market share from terrestrial and satellite radio.

As a result, radio stations are broke. I saw this firsthand when I worked at various radio stations throughout college. One financial radio station had to run a Ponzi scheme to stay afloat (that's a topic for another book). Another radio station, which was owned by Clear Channel, fired someone every month because it couldn't afford to meet its obligations. It started hiring more contractors and commission workers.

Satellite radio isn't doing too hot either. Sirius XM is the one big player in this space because all the other players either went bankrupt or were bought.

Sirius XM's financials aren't very good for an industry leader. I'm not going to get too technical (I have undergrad and Master's degrees in finance and accounting, in addition to journalism and digital broadcasting), but consider this...

A company is generally considered undervalued if it has a price-to-earnings ratio (P/E) well below 20... overvalued if it has a P/E well above 20. Sirius XM (ticker symbol: SIRI) has a P/E over 60, and its stock price is below $3.50 as of this publication (September 2014). That's an overvaluation equivalent to some crappy social media company stocks. So if this stock is very overvalued, and it's priced at below $3.50, then you can estimate how low the real value of Sirius XM is.

Media Business Models

So much media are dependent on advertising for revenue, but advertising models are dying. Advertising should never be a primary revenue driver for any business. The ad industry is changing immensely, and advertisers are becoming more stringent on where and how much they spend on advertising.

Advertisers are now interested in testing campaigns over the short-term. Very few companies want to throw money to improve their brand. It's becoming increasingly difficult to find an advertiser who'll stick with you over the long haul, especially if you're a show on a terrestrial radio station that nobody turns on in his or her car anymore.

Terrestrial radio broadcasters who still think they can make millions from advertising will be sadly disappointed. It's even sadder that some people still think this.

To make money, terrestrial radio stations are charging hosts for airtime. Like advertisers, the people who are paying for airtime will eventually figure out that it's a terrible investment, and they too will leave.

So how can old-school radio stations make money?

They won't be able to. They're toast.

SiriusXM depends heavily on subscriptions from its users, so it's not as reliant on the dying advertising model. If Howard Stern quit broadcasting his Howard Stern Show on SiriusXM, that could be the beginning of the end for SiriusXM. His listeners (he has millions) would probably unsubscribe.

Enter: Podcasting

When I was working terrestrial around 2008, listeners constantly asked why shows weren't in podcast format. They were fed up with setting their alarms to a specific time every day to listen to their favorite shows.

Older radio executives weren't – and still aren't – as up-to-date with the changing digital media landscape. So when I went to them with ideas on how we could have more of an online presence, they ignored me... and then proceeded to fire their workforce to cut costs.

Now, everything is online. If you and your business aren't online, you're leaving money on the table. Terrestrial stations have already lost lots of money. TV stations are doing the same...

all because they didn't do a good job of converging their content online.

As Jason Hartman explained in his foreword, podcasting is the cheapest and easiest way to build an audience and make your voice heard. The radio we're so used to hearing isn't the same medium it was when we were kids. It's a sad fact of reality.

Chapter 2
WHY PODCAST?

Podcasting isn't a new phenomenon, but it hasn't caught on to the mainstream yet. For example, in the HBO series *The Newsroom*, AWM (Atlantis World Media) CEO Leona Lansing (Jane Fonda) threatens to fire anchor Will McAvoy (Jeff Daniels) by saying he is one strike away from hosting his own podcast, as if it's some sort of insult.

Having worked on podcasts for many years now, I can say with certainty that big companies and larger corporations don't see – or know – the value of podcasts yet. It's an easy way to build an audience and engage with it.

This presents a tremendous opportunity.

If AWM released more content in podcast format, AWM wouldn't be facing such budgetary constraints.

According to the Pew Research Center, one in five U.S. adults listens to podcasts occasionally. People listening to podcasts on their cell phones grew 10% from 2010–2012.

Podcasts can be listened to anywhere... at the gym or in the office, while cooking or traveling by car, train, or plane, etc. That's a big market.

When Is It Time To Podcast?

Podcastnomics

The first step in having a successful podcast is picking the proper niche. This is integral. The more targeted the niche, the better.

For example, I met someone a few months ago who's an expert in fixing cars (mechanical problems, tires, paint, etc.). I suggested that he come out with a car mechanics show. Every episode could focus on a specific car issue. He could share all his wisdom.

Put yourself in this guy's shoes...

I searched iTunes and the Internet for "car mechanics" podcasts. About ten shows came up. This isn't great news, but there's still an opportunity here. You can do a better job of providing timelier and better content and steal market share.

You can interview car mechanic experts on your show... just go to Amazon's "Books" section and search for "car mechanic." Hundreds of books pop up. Contact those authors and ask them to be guests on your show.

You can answer questions from listeners who are experiencing issues with their cars. This will help them save money! People love to save money! Especially on their cars. Most mechanics around the corner know the average person knows nothing about cars. So they make their money by scamming customers. I know I'm not the only one who's gotten scammed by a mechanic!

There are many opportunities like this. Once you build your audience and platform, you can start monetizing... through advertising, affiliate marketing, paid (subscription) content, selling your consulting services, selling your car mechanic products, speaking gigs, writing a book, etc.

Podcastnomics

Another hypothetical example...

If you like movies, instead of having a show about movies (there are many of these podcasts), have a show about your favorite movie. Let's say your favorite movie is *Fight Club*. All your podcast episodes will discuss aspects of *Fight Club*.

You might think it's impossible to have more than ten episodes on this topic. That's false. One of my favorite movies is *Requiem for a Dream*. I can probably write a 500-page book on it.

Once you build your audience, the audience will dictate your content. That's when your life as a podcaster becomes easy.

I've built audiences in a matter of two months. And then the audiences would send so much feedback that I didn't have to do any show prep myself.

In a *Fight Club* podcast, you can talk about themes in the movie, specific characters, debate what happened, play out hypothetical scenarios, interview huge fans and experts of the film, the production crew, actors, director, etc.

Who knows... if you gain enough influence, you can get Brad Pitt's attention and interview him. If *Fight Club 2* ever comes out (the sequel to the book will be released in a few years), your show would be the first channel the producers would want to market.

Then you can write an e-book about *Fight Club* and a good chunk of your listeners would buy it... because podcast leads are the highest quality leads on the Internet (more on this later in the book). You can hold "Fight Club" webinars and charge people to attend. You can give keynote speeches at fight clubs around the world.

I've laid out hypothetical examples for you. You can apply the ideas and principles to any of your businesses.

As you'll see while reading this book... podcasting isn't rocket science. There's very little risk in *trying* it.

I'm positive you won't be disappointed... and if you are, e-mail me at naresh dot vissa at gmail dot com and let me know!

Chapter 3
HISTORY OF PODCASTING

The idea of podcasting came about during the 1980s. I'm not going to act as if I know all about podcasting in the 80s because I wasn't even born until the end of the decade. But, the premise is this: back then, only journalists and DJs had any shot of making their actual voices heard. There was no Internet, and everyone and his or her mother subscribed to the local newspaper and listened to terrestrial AM/FM radio.

Because it was impossible for people to create their own content and disseminate it efficiently, people started recording themselves speaking their thoughts on issues. They then shared these recordings with their friends and family.

This was the beginning of podcasting, and it started years before I was born. That's how old the idea is.

As the Internet hit the 90s, people started finding easier and more professional ways to record themselves. They bought nice microphones for their computers. They then were able to record and edit the audio on their computer too. This was called "audioblogging" during the 90s and early 2000s... because people were just aimlessly sharing their thoughts in an audio format.

Digital audio playback devices – like Walkmans and CD players – started getting more advanced. They could hold more space for audio files like mp3s.

In early 2003, a tech evangelist named Dave Winer, who invented the RSS feed ("really simple syndication" in layman's terms) a few years earlier, made it easy to incorporate audio content into an RSS. Previously, only printed text could go in an RSS.

Winer's company, UserLand, added an "enclosure" tag in its RSS. This meant bloggers could now easily link to audio files and be called audiobloggers too.

As these RSS feeds hosted more audio files, space became an issue. In response, content delivery systems and audio hosting services like Liberated Syndication (Libsyn) were created in late 2004.

Apple's iPod made it easy to transfer thousands of audio files onto a pocket-sized digital player. With the iPod, users could listen to audio while driving, running, working, cooking, etc.

Podcastnomics

With amalgamation of audio broadcasting and technology in mind, journalist Ben Hammersley from *The Guardian* dubbed the term "podcasting" in 2004. The term immediately went viral within the audioblogging community.

That's why we now call audioblogs "podcasts".

In 2005, iTunes added a Podcasts section to its Music Store. The podcasters who came out with shows in 2005 and 2006 built up thousands of listeners immediately and ended up making a lot of money since they were first-movers to podcasting on iTunes.

The content delivery systems I mentioned earlier (like Libsyn) beefed up their offerings later in 2005 because podcasters found that exposure to iTunes' huge number of downloaders in its Podcasts section threatened to make great demands on their bandwidth and related expenses. The few hosting providers took off and are now in an oligopoly.

And that's the short history of podcasting. I could go into more details, but only tech nerds (who are not the target audience of this book) would be interested in that.

Chapter 4
SOFTWARE AND EQUIPMENT

Podcasting is not a complicated process. Much of the software and equipment is free and readily available for your use.

Microphone

You'll need a good microphone so you'll sound excellent on-air! A clear-sounding program will come across much better than something that's hard to hear.

I highly recommend the following:

Mac users – Blue Microphone's Snowball USB... this microphone has some of the best sound quality on the market.

Cost: about $55.

Windows users – Audio Technica... there are various versions of this mic. Generally, the more expensive, the better the quality.
Cost: You can get a very high quality Audio Technica mic for less than $40.

USE A FOAM WINDSCREEN to capture and filter sound. Windscreens reduce the occurrence of wind, breath sounds and popping noises. They keep mics clean and extend their lifetimes. Most windscreens fit standard microphones, including the two I mentioned previously.
Cost: $5

To buy equipment, USE AMAZON. Amazon is the one of the best online marketplaces on the Internet. The prices of products these days are INCREDIBLE... thanks to Amazon!

Podcastnomics

NOTE: DO NOT USE THE BUILT-IN MICROPHONE IN YOUR COMPUTER. Built-in mics are okay for casual use, but for professional quality, you'll want to invest in one of the microphones I mentioned.

Bumper Music

Bumper music is the music that plays at the intro and outro of the show. You want to play music that suits the personality of you and your show.

For example, if your show is about hustling to make money and live life, you might want to consider a hip-hop theme. If your show is about spiritualism or God, then you'll want something soft and light-hearted.

Unless you have your own ORIGINAL music, you'll have to use royalty-free music for your shows. My favorite royalty-free provider is Audio

Jungle (www.AudioJungle.net). They have hundreds of thousands of music selections in various genres.

Cost: You can buy a yearly license for as low as $1. For the podcasts I've produced, I've paid about $10 a year per song.

Voiceovers

Voiceovers are those cool voices you hear with the bumper music. Usually, voiceovers are done by a male with a deep voice. It adds coolness and professionalism to your show.

You can hire a true professional to record ten seconds of audio, but he/she will charge you close to $100.

The better alternative: outsource your voiceovers. Go to Fiverr (www.fiverr.com) and search for the highest rated voiceover artists. You can send them your script, and they'll deliver audio files of your voiceovers back to you within a few days.

Cost: $10-$15 for both intros and outros.

Conducting Interviews

Surprisingly, Skype and Google Voice are the easiest high-quality programs you can utilize to do interviews. The connections are generally strong from anywhere in the world, and the audio quality is much better than landline phones.

Cell phones are an absolute no-no. The quality can be so poor that listeners will need to turn up their volumes and pay too much attention just to hear the interview. That's not what you want.

You can use both Google and Skype and make and receive outbound calls as well. They both offer pricing plans.

Price: If you'll be interviewing experts from around the world, then you'll want to purchase the Skype Unlimited World plan (Google calls it something different), which costs $13.99/month... or you can just pay-as-you-go if you don't think you'll be making much calls outside of a weekly interview or two.

Recording

Some paid programs out there are worth purchasing to record your audio. Their quality is excellent!

WINDOWS USERS:

MP3 Skype Recorder (free):
www.voipcallrecording.com

Pamela (paid subscription):
www.pamela.biz

Evaer (paid subscription):

Podcastnomics

www.evaer.com

MAC USERS:

VodBurner (free):

www.vodburner.com

ecamm (the best program for Mac):

www.ecamm.com

These are all great programs (even the free ones).

Editing

Once you have all your software and equipment, editing becomes easy.

MAC USERS: GarageBand is already provided. You can use this to record (more complex to record, so use a recording recommendation I mentioned above) or edit audio.

WINDOWS USERS: Download the free program Audacity to edit music free.

Learning these programs is quite simple... just open the program and play around with it. Record yourself talking and edit some samples yourself.

Hosting

Just as every website domain needs to be hosted in order to go live to the world, so too do podcasts. This is because podcasters in 2005 found that exposure to iTunes' huge number of downloaders in its Podcasts section threatened to make great demands on their bandwidth and related expenses. That's why podcasting entrepreneurs created content delivery systems, or hosting providers.

The hosting provider creates an RSS (stands for "really simple syndication" for non-techies) for your show, which you can then publicize to your listeners to subscribe to. You can also submit the RSS feed link to distributors like iTunes, TuneIn, Stitcher, Spreaker, audioBoom and SoundCloud (more on the importance of these later in the book). People who subscribe to your RSS feed will get automatic updates on new episodes that are released.

The best hosting providers I highly recommend are Liberated Syndication (Libsyn) and SoundCloud.

Assuming you want to treat your podcasting like a business, then you'll want to carefully track your stats. With Libsyn, you get detailed stats of how many downloads and listens your show is getting. With Libsyn's Advanced Stats, you also get geographic information and user agent info on where downloads come from.

That's big.

Most podcasters have no idea where their podcasts will take them. By capturing geographic data (and other qualitative and quantitative metrics), you can better tailor your shows and target your audience for special offers and promotions.

Furthermore, with Libsyn, you can set up your podcast to publish directly to WordPress or Blogger. This makes life incredibly easy once you launch your podcast's website (I recommend you use WordPress).

Other benefits of using Libsyn:

- You can time when episodes go live and even when they do dead. This is convenient when you have travel coming up (or a long holiday) and need to record a bunch of episodes ahead of time.
- You can set up the system to send messages out to your Twitter, Facebook

and LinkedIn accounts when a new episode is live. You can automate this through your account by creating a standard template like, "My latest podcast episode is out! Listen here: (and then the URL will automatically populate)."

- You can get a custom smartphone app for your show. This means the show can be found not just in the podcasting directories – where only about 60 million people a month download podcasts – but also in the app directories where over 1.2 billion people a month download apps.

I've been using Libsyn since I started podcasting, and its data and features have helped me understand the art of podcasting.

Again, you don't have to use Libsyn. The latest up-and-coming hosting service is called SoundCloud, which provides a superior embeddable player and other tidbits.

Whether you go with Libsyn or SoundCloud, you'll be happy with either service. Libsyn has been around longer, so it's what I've been using to host podcasts, but I've heard great things about SoundCloud as well.

SIDE NOTE: Google's FeedBurner does not host media files, but it's great for archiving episodes on the Internet. FeedBurner can be used to *manage* your RSS feed, which has to be created at a service like Libsyn or SoundCloud.

Transcriptions

Transcriptions are print versions of your audio episodes. Some people don't like listening to things. They prefer to read instead. Transcriptions can come in handy for them.

Transcriptions are also GREAT for content generation. You can pick specific segments from your podcasts and post their transcriptions on your website's blog. You can also turn good portions of a podcast into a blog post.

Let's say, for example, you host a podcast dedicated to the movie and book *Fight Club.* Your podcast allows you to reach millions of *Fight Club* fans around the world, including actors Brad Pitt and Edward Norton. Pitt's publicist reaches out to you and asks if he can be interviewed on your show. Your dream has come true! So you interview Pitt.

Now, you want the world to know how cool you are. Your podcast will broadcast to iTunes. But having a print version of the interview – or summarizing the interview into a column or post – brings fantastic SEO value and has the potential of going viral all over the Internet because it's easier to share.

That's what transcripts do... they improve SEO and improve the chances of you and your show spreading.

You can hire transcribers in the U.S. for $50 per 30 minutes of audio. You can hire transcribers overseas for much less than that... as low as $10 per 30 minutes of audio.

I recommend you visit Elance (www.elance.com) and look at their transcription section to find transcribers overseas who will suit your needs and budget.

Cost: $20-$100 per 30 minutes of audio.

Summary

In conclusion, the total start-up cost for a podcast comes out to less than $2,000 for the first year, assuming you get every weekly episode transcribed. Without transcriptions, your start-up cost reduces to less than $300. That's close to nothing!

If you have any questions at all about equipment inquiries or services, contact me at naresh dot vissa at gmail dot com and I'll point you in the right direction.

You can also subscribe to my free newsletter by visiting www.podcastnomics.com.

Chapter 5
HOW TO FORMAT YOUR PODCAST
Part I: The Talk Show

I've talked to so many people who want to start their own podcasts, but they're worried about content. They have no idea what to discuss for even 20 minutes... and then they think about coming out with episodes every week... that's what scares them away.

I wrote this book to explain how easy podcasting can be. Once you have the right equipment (the average person probably has 80% of what's needed to get started), it's only a matter of getting started and actually doing it.

Podcastnomics

A very simple recipe requires minimal work for any podcast. Let me elaborate some more...

A talk show podcast should consist of three segments.

1. Rant of the Day

This is a chance for you to discuss whatever is on your mind. A major reason why people create podcasts is so they have their own soapbox to say whatever they want. If you're reading this book, then you won't have a problem speaking your mind, because you likely have a topic you'd like to podcast on.

To start every show, you can discuss your personal life or something in the news relating to the show's niche.

Estimated duration: 10 minutes maximum

2. Guest Interview

Interviewing an expert in your field (outside of yourself) is so, so important for various reasons.

First, it brings an entirely new voice and perspective to the show, even if the guest agrees with you on everything. Your listeners will get tired of hearing your voice and your opinion, so bringing in an authority will keep the audience engaged.

Secondly, big-name guests can help superbly with SEO and driving new traffic to your podcast and podcast's site. All guests want to brag to their followers (their mailing list subscribers, social media followers, etc.) that they were interviewed or featured by the media... even if it's just a small podcast with 1,000 listeners. They will link to your episode and send *their* assets *your* way.

THIS IS BIG!

In the next chapter, I'll explain more on how you can go about finding guests and booking them on your show.

Estimated duration: 15-20 minutes

3. Feedback

What's the point of having your own show and not conversing with the people who listen to you?

You need to make it as easy as possible for people to find and contact you (more on people finding your podcast in the chapter titled, "HOW TO EXECUTE YOUR PODCAST MARKETING").

This means:

- Create profiles for all social media, particularly a Facebook page, Twitter handle, and LinkedIn company page. If your show involves visual stimuli – like if it's about cars or girls – then you'll definitely want an Instagram account with frequently uploaded pictures.

- Create a YouTube channel. Upload all your podcasts on to this channel. You can upload them as movie files and have a still photo with your podcast's information, such as its name, site, social media and contact info. This not only gives people more ways to listen, but they can comment and send you messages too.

- Have a hotline number where people can leave voice-mails.

- Create a feedback e-mail address. For example, my feedback for a podcast on this book is naresh dot vissa at gmail dot com.

- Create a Google Alert for you and your show. If you don't know how to do this, just Google "Google Alerts" and you can walk through the process of setting up Alerts. You will be notified every time anything is written on the Internet about you or your podcast. You'll just need to supply Google with the exact key words it should scrape. On your podcasts, definitely respond to alerts on your show whenever something is written about you.

You can then read ALL the feedback you get... through social media, YouTube, e-mail, voice-mail, iTunes comments, Google Alerts, etc. After a few months of podcasting, you'll realize there's *so much* feedback that you can spend hours responding to it all. You can do entire shows that are based solely on listener feedback.

Answering listener questions and comments is always entertaining and makes for great content.

Estimated duration: 15 minutes maximum

That's it. You can create a nearly one-hour podcast just by sticking to the recipe of these three segments.

The only segment that requires a few minutes of effort is the guest interview. You'll have to contact, book the guest, and do a little research on his or her background. But outside of that, conducting these requires little prep and can be done on the fly.

Side Notes:

Each of the segments listed above can be their own podcast... so you can just have a podcast filled with episodes consisting of ten-minute rants or a podcast consisting of short five-minute episodes where you answer one listener question per episode.

There is no precise formula to how to format your podcast... just be creative in your thinking.

Podcastnomics

Another format you can try – but is extremely difficult to pull off – is the investigative news magazine style podcast. The *Freakonomics Radio* podcast is a perfect example of this. To execute this, however, you need a huge budget to hire seasoned producers. *Freakonomics Radio* gets public funding, which is why it can produce such high-quality podcasts with amazing coverage and stories.

Duration

DO NOT GO PAST ONE HOUR. Listeners can give you their attention for so long, so once you hit the 50-minute mark, get ready to wrap up your show.

Shorter talk show format podcasts are fine too. As a podcaster, you won't face hard stops or editorial restrictions. Research from Stitcher suggests that 22 minutes of audio is the optimal time for a listener to give their full attention.

Chapter 6
HOW TO FORMAT YOUR PODCAST
Part II: The Reader

The previous chapter discussed the format of a podcast talk show. There's another way you can start a successful podcast with very little work. It's incredibly simple for people who have blogs or for publishers that write or report information.

The idea is to launch an audio version of your blog posts, free e-letters, articles, etc. This is super simple to produce. All you have to do is read print content you've already produced. Many print media and newspapers are already doing this. This costs even less than doing a talk show and takes *way* less time.

Podcastnomics

More and more people are turning to audio forms of content. They want to listen to something educational during their drives, runs, and work. If you don't believe me, then just Google Audible's sales performance and read the various articles that discuss how much it's growing.

Chapter 7
HOW TO FORMAT YOUR PODCAST
Part III: The Interview Podcast

The "interview podcast" consists of nothing but interviews with guests. This isn't a bad way to go about podcasting, but it comes with limitations.

The point in podcasting is to build up an audience, and more importantly, to *build rapport* with your listeners. If you're just interviewing other experts every episode and not spending any time talking to your audience, they won't be able to build virtual trust with you. As a result, it'll be harder for them to take *you* seriously and harder for you to sell yourself and any further products.

Podcastnomics

I've worked with many podcasts that just did interviews with people. They hired me to be their booker and just schedule a ton of guests. Some worked out... most didn't. Many of the big-name guests who are interviewed are also quoted or referenced by hundreds of other media every month. What makes you and your reporting any different?

The "interview podcasts" I worked on that did work out were ones that were part of a broader network of podcasts. For example, Jason Hartman (who wrote the foreword to this book) has a network of nearly 20 podcasts. It's okay for him to have 15 shows that just interview guests, because each podcast is about a very specialized, niche topic, like survivalism or life extension. Interviews are okay for these because the audience is already extremely focused. Jason still builds rapport and gets himself out there by providing commentary on his specialties and general life in the other podcasts he does that aren't solely guest interviews.

***

You don't want to have a "general" podcast where you interview a bunch of experts from different subject areas. Talking to a star athlete about fitness one day and then talking to the CEO of a tech company about his firm's financials on the next episode won't develop a consistency, and therefore, will not bode well with your listeners. It doesn't matter if both guests are big-name celebrities.

If you're hoping to start a killer podcast that will make you a leader in your space and some money in the process, then you want to share your personality *and* interview guests who will market you. The "interview podcast" can get you started, but it won't do enough to get you to where you want to be.

Chapter 8
HOW TO FIND GUESTS FOR YOUR SHOW

Booking guests can sound daunting and time-consuming, but with a few weeks of practice, it'll actually become a fun and worthwhile exercise for you.

Here are some ideas on how you can go about finding and contacting prospective experts to join your podcast:

1. Join media databases so you're being pitched on relevant experts.

Joining media databases will put you (and your e-mail address) into various distribution lists. It will also make it easy for publicists to contact you.

You can choose to get e-mail from targeted niches. For example, since most of the shows I produce are financial in nature, I choose to receive only business-related pitches.

Cision, Gorkana, Vocus, Burrelles Luce, and My Media Info are my favorite media databases that frequently send me PR pitches. Google these companies and join them immediately!

2. Use Amazon to find authors who have written about your niche topic.

If your niche is basket weaving, then type in "basket weaving" in Amazon's "Books" category. You'll see hundreds of books that come up on basket weaving.

Click the names of the authors and Google them as well as their companies' names. You'll be able to find their personal or companies' websites. Most of these sites will have "Contact Us" tabs that will allow you to contact them.

If they don't have "Contact Us" tabs, then you can go to www.WhoIs.com and paste the URL and search for the website's backend information. In this information, you'll find the web URL administrator's e-mail address. Most of the time, this is the e-mail of the guest you're looking for. After this, you'll have all the info you need to invite people to come on your podcast.

Very few people you find on Amazon will turn you down. Heavy-hitting guests might decline because of their time constraints, but other middle-of-the-pack experts will be honored to be on your show.

3. Subscribe free to HARO (Help A Reporter Out).

www.HelpAReporter.com

HARO is a platform that connects journalists with sources. It sends out three e-mails a day with pitches *from journalists* (not publicists) who give an overview of the stories they're working on and the sources they need.

To get guests on your podcast, you can join HARO at the link above and submit queries for expert guests on your podcast. Make sure it includes:

- Background of show
- Who you are
- Type of expert you're looking to interview
- If you have had big-name guests on the podcast, then include their names to build your credibility

- Any other information you deem as important

No joke... an hour after posting one query, you will receive hundreds of e-mails back from assistants, marketing assistants, publicists, and experts. This can be a problem, but it's a good problem to have... just make sure you properly perform your due diligence in vetting any potential guests. Visit their websites. Look at the books they've written on Amazon. See if they've been on other media by Googling their name or searching Google News.

4. Search for other podcasts in your niche on iTunes.

Open the Podcasts section in iTunes, and just search your niche.

If your niche is running, then type in "running" or "marathon training." If your niche is "crowdfunding," then type in "crowdfunding."

See what pops up. If there are other shows in your niche, then look at the guests who were on those shows. They'll likely want to be guests on your show too.

Additionally, look at the hosts of the shows in your niche. Invite the hosts to be guests on your show. There's a very good chance the host will return the favor and ask you to be a guest on his/her show as well. The comingling is great for marketing purposes: the host will get access to your listeners, and you will get access to the host's listeners too.

5. While prepping for your show, make note of experts the media quotes.

Podcastnomics

Chances are you are an expert in the niche you're podcasting about, and you've become an expert because you have read and watched a lot of material on your niche.

In my case, I've become well versed on business and entrepreneurship. I subscribe to various newsletters and trade publications and closely follow experts within the field.

By staying in touch with my niches, I am introduced to experts every day. All it takes is a Google search of their names to get in touch with them.

Chapter 9
HOW TO CONTACT POTENTIAL GUESTS

N ow that you've found experts to interview, it's time to get in touch.

E-mail is best. You can call, but experts and publicists don't want to take 50 calls a day from media producers. They'll all tell you to send them an e-mail.

When contacting guests, keep in mind that these are working-class individuals who are devoted to their jobs. Give them many dates and times to record so they can come back promptly with a confirmation.

Podcastnomics

I've pasted a sample template below of what you can e-mail experts to get them to come on your show. Include:

- Your name, title and affiliation
- Info on your show (description, website, etc.)
- Awesome facts about your show to get the guest hyped (stats, countries, famous guests who have been on)
- A couple of dates and times to record

The key is... you want to hype you and your shows up to MAKE the guest want to come on.

SUBJECT: [SHOW NAME] Interview Request

BODY:

[NAME OF GUEST OR PUBLICIST],

I am a producer for [SHOW NAME]. Our show offers innovative, forward-thinking strategies, and we believe your knowledge is ideal for one of our upcoming episodes.

We can accommodate you at [TIMES] on [TWO DATES TO RECORD].

Our shows has a global audience in [NUMBER] countries (check your Libsyn stats to see how many downloads and countries) and are frequently ranked at the top of iTunes. Previous guests have included [LIST FAMOUS GUESTS WHO HAVE BEEN ON YOUR SHOW].

[INCLUDE 2-3 SENTENCES ABOUT WHAT THE SHOW COVERS]

It is our goal to supply our listeners with the best and brightest guests who can give insight into [STATE YOUR NICHE] as well as lifestyle choices. Our audience knows all too well how important education, hard work and knowledge are in shaping the future.

Please feel free to check out our exclusive site here: [URL OF WEBSITE]

I sincerely hope you can join us on our show. I thank you for your consideration and will look forward to your reply.

Thanks.

[SIGNATURE]

Chapter 10
THE IMPORTANCE OF iTUNES

The idea of podcasting really isn't anything revolutionary. A podcast is essentially a radio show... nothing groundbreaking there.

BUT THE ONLY REASON WHY PODCASTING IS A VENTURE WORTH PURSUING FOR BUSINESSES IS BECAUSE OF iTUNES.

iTunes has changed the game. iTunes has spent a lot of money and resources to create a podcast functionality, and in return, podcasting has turned into a profitable and worthwhile venture.

Podcastnomics

iTunes' podcasting platform makes Apple a lot of money.

iTunes allows podcasters to get out in front of the world... just like Amazon allows authors to sell their books.

Leads

Why is iTunes so big for podcasting? Think about it...

Think about all the people who own an iPhone or iPad or Mac... really any Apple product. And then realize that the "Podcasts" app automatically comes with all of these products.

The new iOS 8 integrates the Podcast app natively onto Apple products. This will be the turning point for podcasting. Hundreds of millions of people will be getting this app around the globe, and they won't be able to delete it.

Will every Apple user use the "Podcasts" app? No. But already, Apple is helping market its podcasting platform to the masses.

Now think about the types of people who own Apple products... we're talking about folks who have some tech savvy and money to spend.

The moment a user "Subscribes" to a podcast on iTunes, they have committed to receive all of a podcast's episodes indefinitely. This means they actually *want* to listen to every show. And it means this user is highly qualified. They're likely educated, working-class or studying, and have money to spend to improve themselves.

THIS IS THE ULTIMATE LEAD. NO OTHER MARKETING CHANNEL WILL PROVIDE HIGHER QUALITY LEADS.

In essence, Apple already does the filtering for podcasters. It's just up to you to come out with consistent and quality content and distribute it effectively.

iTunes Rankings

iTunes has rankings for its podcast categories. Its categories include:

- Arts
- Business
- Comedy
- Education
- Health
- Music
- Religion & Spirituality
- Sports & Recreation
- Technology

Every category has subcategories. For example, the "Sports & Recreation" section has sub-categories like "Outdoor" and "Professional." The subcategory I've used a lot within the "Business" section is "Investing."

All categories and subcategories are ranked NUMERICALLY.

According to my source with inside access to iTunes, the rankings are based on an algorithm equivalent to the number of subscribers podcasts get over a 2-3 week period.

This means that other user experience functionalities – such as comments and ratings – DON'T MATTER. All that matters is that you get users to hit the SUBSCRIBE button on iTunes.

So when you're telling your friends, social media followers, and other people about your show, TELL THEM TO FIND YOUR SHOW ON iTUNES AND SUBSCRIBE.

Podcastnomics

The greater your ranking, the more "free advertising" you're getting from the iTunes Store. For example, random people looking for podcasts on investing will see mainstream names like Jim Cramer, Dave Ramsey and the Motley Fool at the top of the "Investing" rankings. But if you start your own investing podcast and make a big push (as I did with one of my clients), then it will catch up to the top of those mainstream names. People get tired of listening to mainstream names, so they'll give the unknown show with the high ranking a shot. That's how you bring in new listeners.

Again, keep in mind all the millions of people globally who use iTunes. And imagine your show being #1 on the rankings. It's a great way to market your show... completely free of charge.

I utilized this strategy with my clients... to rise the rankings on iTunes... and the results were incredible. We were able to bring in completely new leads to our businesses, and then we converted those leads into paying customers.

Google has search engine optimizers (SEO experts). Does iTunes have iTunes optimizers?

I know a black hat hacker who does iTunes optimization. He will make sure your show rises the iTunes rankings. But it's illegal and risky. Apple (and Google) has no tolerance for black hat tricks, so if they ever find out, you and your business will be banned for life.

In addition to publishing podcast rankings, iTunes has "What's Hot" and "New & Noteworthy" sections. Again, being featured on these sections would be free advertising.

"New & Noteworthy"

Pretty much every new podcast is featured in "New & Noteworthy." The question is… how long will a new podcast be featured?

The more content you pump out as soon as you launch your podcast on iTunes, the longer it'll be featured on the "New & Noteworthy" section. If you can come out with fresh content every day, there's a good chance your podcast will be featured for AS LONG AS TWO MONTHS.

This is one of those rare cases where *quantity is greater than quality*. It doesn't matter if each episode is less than five minutes long. Keep releasing new content to keep your audience engaged. iTunes algorithms will take notice.

"What's Hot"

To make "What's Hot," your podcast needs to get a lot of downloads and listens. While the

Rankings depend on the number of users who subscribe, and "New & Noteworthy" depends on quantity of episodes, "What's Hot" depends on actual performance of the podcast. The more downloads and listens the podcast gets, the better.

iTunes has implemented an algorithm that considers average and overall performance. That way, even if you're a new podcaster, if your first episode is a home run, you will be featured on "What's Hot."

THIS IS WHY IT'S SO IMPORTANT TO COME OUT WITH A LOT OF HIGH QUALITY CONTENT AS SOON AS YOU LAUNCH YOUR PODCAST.

The easiest way to generate buzz with your first couple of episodes is by interviewing big name guests who will market for you. This could be a big name guest with a large following on social media or other media – like Tim Ferriss or

James Altucher – or a big name guest who the public cares about – like Jay-Z or Barack Obama.

When I launched an investing podcast for a client back in 2011, our first guest was Jim Rogers, who's one of the richest hedge fund investors in the world. For whatever reason, people – especially free market supporters – love what Jim Rogers has to say. No matter who interviews him, the hit ends up going viral.

We interviewed Mr. Rogers on the podcast, and it generated more than 30,000 downloads and listens within 24 hours. The name brand of "Jim Rogers" did all the marketing for us.

We were featured on the "New & Noteworthy," "What's Hot," and "Top Episodes" rankings. This was a great start to our podcast and set the stage for much success for the podcasting venture.

Chapter 11
HOW TO SUBMIT A PODCAST TO iTUNES

Once you have your RSS created (through Libsyn, as mentioned earlier in the book), you can submit your podcast's feed to iTunes for distribution in iTunes and through the Podcasts app.

The steps to do this are quick and simple:

1. Download and open the latest version of iTunes.
2. On the top right, click the iTunes Store button.
3. Click "Podcasts" on the navigation bar.

4. On the right, below the Podcast Quick Links header, click "Submit a Podcast."

5. Follow the instructions on the "Submit a Podcast" page to submit your podcast

iTunes Logo

For iTunes, you definitely want to have a colorful and catchy logo. Generally, design elements like logos aren't important, but on a platform like iTunes, where thousands of podcasts compete with each other, something catchy will make a difference.

The logo will need to be 1400x1400 pixels.

Title Of Your Show

On iTunes, you'll want to include as many key words as possible in your subtitle. This is because the more key words you have, the greater the chance you'll be found by a user.

On your podcast's website (not iTunes), you can change the subtitles up so everything flows better. But on iTunes, the important thing is that you include as many key words as you can so you can be found.

I just made up this title off of the top of my head, but pay particular attention to the key words, which I've bolded. It's not the greatest sounding title in the world, but it'll do for iTunes:

GET RICH NOW: Using Investing and Economics to Live Healthy

When someone types in any of these terms, your show will now be included in the results. If you get enough subscribers, then you'll be one of the first podcasts that pops up.

Chapter 12
HOW TO EXECUTE YOUR PODCAST MARKETING

If you execute your podcast properly and run it like a business, then the marketing will take care of itself.

The previous sentence is so important to follow, so I'll write it again.

IF YOU EXECUTE YOUR PODCAST PROPERLY AND RUN IT LIKE A BUSINESS, THEN THE MARKETING WILL TAKE CARE OF ITSELF.

Here's a recipe for success that will help you execute and market effectively.

1. Become an early mover in a niche.

There are millions of niches out there. Be a part of a long tail.

My technical background is in finance. Right now, the growing niches are digital currencies and crowdfunding. When I type in these key words into the iTunes podcast section, very little comes up. This means there are opportunities!

You can create a podcast on anything. A podcast is an audio blog. So if you love Air Jordan shoes, start a podcast on Air Jordans! That's quite niche.

If you love something enough, you'll never run out of stuff to talk about.

2. Release frequent content early in the process.

The more content you pump out as soon as you launch your podcast on iTunes, the longer it'll be featured on the "New & Noteworthy" section. If you can come out with fresh content every day, there's a good chance your podcast will be featured for as long as two months.

This is one of those rare cases where quantity is greater than quality. It doesn't matter if each episode is less than five minutes long. Keep releasing new content to keep your audience engaged. iTunes algorithms will take notice.

After a couple of months of pumping out frequent content, cool down the publishing to once a week. Why only once? Sometimes, less is more. If you release something every day of the year, it could become difficult for listeners to keep track. Any sense of anticipation would be removed.

By posting once a week, you keep listeners waiting for what's next. This ensures they'll focus *more* on each episode that is released.

SO IF YOU'RE RELEASING AN EPISODE ONCE A WEEK, WHICH DAY IS BEST TO PUBLISH?

Definitely have a set publishing schedule so your listeners know when to look out for your podcast. Your favorite TV show comes on a certain day and time every week. Do the same with your podcast.

Tuesday is when new music releases in the iTunes Store. This means there is lots of traffic on iTunes on Tuesday.

3. Use all distribution networks.

iTunes is the largest and most effective platform to distribute podcasts. But there are others out there that will give your podcast even more publicity. All you have to do is create a profile and submit your RSS to get your podcast into each platform's system for distribution.

I can explain each one, but that's not important. It would be more efficient to just list the ones I use:

- iTunes
- TuneIn (www.tunein.com)
- Stitcher (www.stitcher.com)
- Spreaker (www.spreaker.com)
- SoundCloud (www.soundcloud.com)
- audioBoom (www.audioboom.com)
- PodOmatic (www.podomatic.com)
- PodBean (www.podbean.com)
- Podbay (www.podbay.fm)

- Blubrry (www.blubrry.com)
- RawVoice (www.rawvoice.com)
- Player FM (www.player.fm)

These distributors all have their own users and subscribers. They are great for SEO. The more you get your podcast out there, the better the chance of it going noticed.

4. Create a separate website that captures leads and publishes all podcasts.

This is SO important. Too many podcast managers just publish their shows on iTunes and do nothing else. The point of iTunes is to bring in new listeners. But you'll then want to funnel those listeners into your network so you can directly engage with them.

By engage, I mean you'll want to post blog articles on your site or send listeners e-mails on: episode updates, upcoming guests, thoughts on shows or guests, schedule changes, marketing and sales messages, happy holiday greetings, etc.

Publishing episodes on your website gives listeners a chance to listen to your episodes in a different way. Not everyone likes iTunes. In fact, I listen to all of my favorite podcasts by visiting the official websites of the podcasts. I rarely use iTunes... but that's just me.

You want to give all listeners and potential listeners every possible way to find and listen to your show.

A controversial or newsworthy interview can go viral if it's posted on a website... not on iTunes.

There are just so many pros to having a fully functional website for your podcast. The website will help collect listener e-mails, but it will also be great for search engine optimization (SEO).

Big-name guests will help with Google search and rankings.

5. Grow Your Mailing List.

The easiest way to engage with your audience outside of your podcast is by having a website with a free newsletter mailing list. MailChimp is the easiest and quickly becoming the most common e-mail service provider (ESP). I use it for my businesses and love its features. And it's very cheap compared to competitors like AWeber, Salesforce, iContact and Infusionsoft.

To capture names, make sure you have plenty of newsletter opt-in boxes and maybe even a pop-up asking visitors to subscribe to your free mailing list so they can stay up to date on your latest episodes. I've even had clients force users to enter their e-mail in order to listen to any podcast on the site. For example, when clicking the "Play" button or clicking "Listen" on a site, a pop-up comes up immediately asking the user to enter their e-mail into a box so they can listen to the episode they clicked on. This seems forceful, but it's a great way to collect new e-mail leads.

THE QUICKEST WAY TO GET YOUR EXISTING LISTENERS TO JOIN YOUR MAILING LIST IS TO "GIVE AWAY" SOMETHING OF VALUE FREE OF CHARGE. Below are items you can give away your site's visitors for free:

- Special report
- E-book
- Special audio segment
- One-year free trial to your product
- Free consultation

You want to tease your giveaway on-air. Tell the audience clearly what you're giving away, why it's of value, and how they can take advantage of your offer.

Here's an example of what you can say:

"I wrote a brand new e-book on how to make a million dollars from one single weekly podcast. To find out all my strategies and secrets, visit www.milliondollarpodcast.com [completely made that up] and enter your e-mail in the opt-in box. We'll immediately send you the e-book via e-mail completely free of charge. That's www.milliondollarpodcast.com. It's free. The book is a quick read. This will be well-worth your time."

For one former client, I ran a campaign where we gave away free digital subscriptions to a paid newsletter if people entered their e-mail on a landing page we created in a vanity URL. We built our mailing list to more than 10,000 subscribers from scratch over a one-month period because of this campaign.

6. Interview guests.

The easiest way to generate buzz for your podcast is by interviewing big name guests whose name will do the marketing for you. This could be a big name guest with a large following on social media or other media – like Tim Ferriss or James Altucher – or a big name guest who the public cares about – like Jay-Z or Kim Kardashian.

AS SOON AS YOU LAUNCH YOUR PODCAST, *MAKE SURE* YOUR FIRST GUESTS ARE *TOP-NOTCH.* THIS WILL GET iTUNES TO MARKET YOU SENSATIONALLY!

When I launched an investing podcast for a client back in 2011, our first guest was Jim Rogers, who's one of the richest hedge fund investors in the world. For whatever reason, investors and economists – especially free market supporters – love what Jim Rogers has to say. No matter who interviews him, the hit ends up going viral.

We interviewed Mr. Rogers on the podcast, and it generated more than 40,000 downloads and listens within 24 hours. The name brand of "Jim Rogers" did all the marketing for us.

We were featured on the "New & Noteworthy," "What's Hot," and "Top Episodes" rankings. This was a great start to our podcast and set the stage for much success for the podcasting venture.

In addition, use iTunes to find other podcasts within your niche. Look at the hosts of the shows in your niche. Invite the hosts to be guests on your show. There's a very good chance the host will return the favor and ask you to be a guest on his/her show as well. The comingling is great for marketing purposes: the host will get access to your listeners, and you will get access to the host's listeners too.

7. Send guests links to their episodes.

MAKE SURE YOU SEND YOUR GUESTS THEIR EPISODES AFTER THEY'RE PUBLISHED. This is so imperative because the guests will want to brag about their appearance on your show to their subscribers, followers, friends, family, etc. They will e-mail it to their lists. They will post it on all their social media.

This is exactly what you want.

Your website gives your guests the chance to link to your site on their site, mailing list, social media, etc. It's easier to link to an episode page on a website than on a single episode on iTunes. Guests can drive their following and traffic to your site, and then you can convert them to leads, and hopefully, to loyal listeners.

The guests will remember you more if you engage with them after the interview – through social media, a thank-you gift, or a short follow-up e-mail with the episode page's link. Media guests do so many interviews. Some do thousands of interviews every year. By following up and engaging with them, you won't be just another podcast host who lives in his parents' basement.

The guest might even refer more guests within their industry to you in the future. He or she might also send you free stuff (conference tickets, books, etc.).

You want to start and maintain as many relationships with guests as you can, so don't hesitate to friend them on Facebook, follow them on Twitter, or add them on LinkedIn. You never know what the guest can do for you in the future... whether it's recommending your show publicly or becoming a potential business partner. These networking tactics have helped my clients and me immensely!

8. Convert audio podcasts into print content to improve SEO and shareability.

Transcriptions are GREAT for content generation. You can pick specific segments from your podcasts and post their transcriptions on your website's blog. You can also turn good portions of a podcast into blog posts.

Let's say, for example, you host a podcast dedicated to the movie and book *Fight Club*. Your podcast allows you to reach millions of *Fight Club* fans around the world, including actors Brad Pitt and Edward Norton. Pitt's publicist reaches out to you and asks if he can be interviewed on your show. Your dream has come true! So you interview Pitt.

Now, you want the world to know how cool you are. And then other people can share how cool you are through social media.

The audio version of your podcast will be broadcast on iTunes and other distributors, but having a print version of the interview – or summarizing the interview into a column or post – brings marvelous SEO value and has the potential of going viral all over the Internet because it is easier to share.

That's what transcripts can do... they improve SEO and enhance the chances of you and your show spreading. They give you great ideas for print content. And since you'll already have the transcript (you can hire someone as mentioned earlier or do it yourself), actually writing a watered down piece becomes easy. It shouldn't take longer than a half-hour.

9. Incorporate YouTube and social media into marketing strategy.

Build followings on social media so people can share your show with their networks. Post all your episodes on YouTube, Facebook, Twitter, Myspace, Pinterest pictures, etc.

Give your audience of followers what they want. Post updates, respond to public and private messages, read feedback on-air. Do whatever you need to do to stay active and engaged on social media.

Congratulate loyal social media followers publicly. Your audience will get a kick out of it. It'll convey a sense of realness.

Focus extra on YouTube, because it's such a widely used content sharing platform. Create a YouTube channel. Upload all your podcasts on to this channel. You can upload them as movie files and just have a still photo with your podcast's information, such as its name, site, social media and contact info. This not only gives people more ways to listen, but they can comment and send you messages too.

Social media has real *intangible* value. Social media won't make you much money, but it'll increase your podcast's brand, awareness and engagement greatly. It's awesome for customer service. It also leaves several doors open for an episode or blog post to go viral. These days, nothing can go viral without social media.

***

In summary:

- Become an early mover in a niche.
- Release frequent content.
- Use all distribution networks.

- Create a separate website that captures leads and makes the podcasts available.

- Grow your mailing list.

- Interview guests and send them links to their episodes.

- Send guests links to their episodes.

- Convert audio podcasts into print content to improve SEO and shareability.

- Incorporate YouTube and social media into marketing strategy.

There are many podcasts that fail, but that's largely because several of the steps above are missing in their execution.

To get strategies like the above delivered straight to your inbox, visit this book's website at www.podcastnomics.com and subscribe to the free mailing list.

Chapter 13
REVENUE DRIVERS FOR YOUR PODCAST

Now that I've explained how to start up and manage podcasts, this chapter provides a blueprint to actually monetize them.

In the previous chapter "How To Execute Your Podcast Marketing," I discussed strategies to market your podcasts to bring in listeners and new leads to your business. Now, it's time to use those leads to make money.

I've spoken at length about the high value of podcast listeners and iTunes subscribers. Below are three core revenue drivers that EVERY podcast should implement:

1. Selling an existing product

Podcasting is great for funneling in leads so you can sell them something.

You can sell:

- Books
- Consulting services
- Whatever your business sells
- Other people's products (if you work out a deal for them to pay you)

If you interview authors on your show, then work out deals to sell their books. You can ask for a 50-75% cut for any books you sell through your podcast. Amazon has an affiliate program to track sales.

If you're interviewing an expert who has a product to sell, then ask him or her if you can sell it for them. 100% of your guests will appreciate your asking.

Here are some ways you can sell products through a podcast:

A. Send a sales e-mail to your mailing list.

Numerous studies have shown that an e-mail loses its luster after 24 hours, so this is the quickest and most direct way to make a buck. You will see sales pour in immediately.

B. Post the affiliate tracking link to your episode page and social media.

Your episode page has a pass-along effect. People will be able to find your site years down the road. This means there's always a chance your product will be sold in perpetuity.

C. Have banners on your site marketing your product.

The banners can take clickers straight to a product overview page with a short order form.

D. Create a vanity URL to plug on the podcast so you can track sales.

Announce the URL on-air so listeners have a clear call to action. The vanity URL can host a short order form or longer promotional copy to sell whatever product you'd like.

E. Create space ad text inserts in your print content.

Space ads, or text inserts, are ads blatantly thrown into print content. The idea is to throw off the reader by *inserting* something that relates to the content and will get their attention.

Below is an example of how a space ad can be formatted and inserted into a blog post:

> "Hello my name is Naresh. I am the author of *Podcastnomics*. I spent a few months writing the book. It was a challenge to write and publish it.

> The Mayans were a few years late... 2014 will be the end!

> Click here to listen to a podcast that explains how you can protect yourself NOW!

> I didn't write *Podcastnomics* with the hopes of making a million dollars in royalties. I just love writing and talking about podcasts.

Podcasting can be a very fun and lucrative part of any business. I highly recommend you give it a shot today."

In the above example, the section about the Mayans is the space ad.

2. Premium (paid) podcast content

In addition to your free podcast that will be available everywhere, you can also release a subscription product that listeners would have to pay for. Charge $10 a month (or more), and give subscribers many valuable goodies, such as:

- Special interviews
- Controversial episodes that can't be distributed to a free audience (because of offensive nature or something else that needs to be kept under the wraps)

- Episodes where you give away big secrets
- Off-topic episodes on life or anything else listeners want to hear

When I launched a premium podcast in the financial space for a large financial publisher, our offerings included:

- Two stock picks a month delivered in podcast format, with thorough commentary, analysis and questioning
- One special monthly business episode on a non-financial topic (like entrepreneurship, numismatics, stamp collecting, etc.)
- One off-topic show where hosts got drunk and ranted about life

For $10 a month, those offerings were a steal, considering the financial publisher charged about $10 a month for just one issue of a stock-picking newsletter that gave just one recommendation.

Put together a bundled package that will entice listeners to buy a subscription to your premium podcast. You'll be surprised at how many of your loyal listeners will want to buy anything from you.

3. Advertising

Advertising includes banners and space ads on your website, marketing e-mails to your list, and audio commercials on your podcasts. It also includes products you plug for your affiliates (trusted partners), whom will pay you for any items of theirs that you sell through your assets.

The easiest way to get advertisers is by contacting the biggest companies in your niche. For example, if you have a podcast on fast food eateries, then contact Yum Brands, McDonald's, or Starbucks and see if they'll advertise. If I wanted to start a podcast on digital currencies, then I'd contact the big players in the space: SecondMarket, Coinbase, BitPay, etc.

I listen to about ten hours' worth of podcasts every week. Three larger companies that seem to be very open to advertising on all podcasts are:

- Squarespace
- Hulu
- Audible

If you want them – or any other business – to advertise on your podcast, simply visit their website and contact them. They might have an "Advertising" section on their site that gives you more info too.

Podcastnomics

Advertising can keep a podcast solvent. The most I ever made through podcast advertising was $20,000 a month over a period of a couple of months. But then both advertisers pulled their ads for various reasons. Nevertheless, advertising is always an option... it's just the stability in ad revenue won't always be there.

Advertising should never be a primary revenue driver. The ad industry is changing immensely, and advertisers are becoming more stringent on where and how much they spend on advertising.

Advertisers are now interested in testing campaigns over the short-term. Very few companies want to throw money to improve their brand. It's becoming increasingly difficult to find an advertiser who'll stick with you over the long haul, especially if you're just another small, niche podcast.

It's easier to track data through technological advancements that weren't available 20 years ago.

Don't believe me? Try this...

Write down two ads you saw on any newsprint or website you visited over the past week. These could be ads in physical papers or magazines... or banners or space insert ads on sites.

If you remember those ads, did you visit the website being advertised, dial the call to action number, or click on the links?

My estimate is that 99% of you didn't.

This exercise requires you to:

1) Remember ads after time has lapsed
2) Actually follow-up on the ads

Podcastnomics

Very few people can do both things above because the ads aren't targeted. Only online media businesses with lots of money can target, like Facebook, Twitter, Google, etc... not small podcasts like us. The ads also aren't directly marketed to reach readers. They're just thrown on a broadsheet and carry little meaning or thought into how they can actually help readers.

With that being said, your podcast and its site will already have a niche audience and following built up, so the advertising – as long as it relates to your niche – can be successful. Again, I just want to paint you the picture in the preceding paragraphs of the current advertising landscape.

If you release your podcast thinking you'll become a millionaire by selling a bunch of ads... then don't podcast.

***

In summary, any podcast can implement these revenue drivers to make money:

1. Selling an existing product
2. Premium (paid) podcast content
3. Advertising

I've laid out a blueprint... you'll just have to do a little bit of additional thinking on making it work for your individual situation.

If you have any questions, e-mail me at naresh dot vissa at gmail dot com. Be sure to subscribe to my free newsletter mailing list at www.podcastnomics.com.

STAY IN TOUCH

Tweet me @xnareshx.

Visit www.podcastnomics.com to subscribe to my free newsletter mailing list.

If you have any questions, e-mail me at naresh dot vissa at gmail dot com.

Please go to Amazon and review this book!

AFTERWORD

By Rob Walch, Vice President of Podcaster Relations at Libsyn

Podcasting has gone through three major inflection points in its history. The first was in June 2005, when Apple launched support for podcasting in iTunes. That brought podcasting into the public eye on mass for the first time. However, podcasts were still niche and difficult to consume.

The second inflection point (really a turning point) started two years later in June 2007 with the launch of the iPhone. The original iPhone ushered in the age of the modern smartphone. As mass adoption of smartphones took off, so did podcasting. By June 2014, mobile represented over 64% of podcast downloads vs. just 43% 18 months earlier. Those with a modern smartphone can consume podcasts directly on their mobile devices – no syncing to a computer required – but users still needed to download an app to consume podcasts, and they needed to know such an app existed before they could download it.

The third inflection point was in September 2014 when Apple launched iOS 8 – and it had the Podcasts app installed natively in iOS for the first time. By the end of October 2014, there were over half a billion people with the Podcasts app on their iOS device. This number will grow to be close to one billion people by the end of 2015, and that is just on the iOS side. Podcasting is now entering into its true golden age of mass adoption.

There are many good reasons on why you should podcast – many of which were covered well in this book.

- Brand Building

- More time in the day for someone to listen to audio than read a blog or watch a video
- Higher level of engagement with your customers / audience
- Conveys a higher level of authority than a simple blog
- Getting your content into iTunes where there are no blogs
- Podcast listeners = more sales and leads
- The spoken word carries more emotion than the written word

Yes – they are all good reasons to podcast. But in my opinion, the best reason is a simple one, and one that has always been a key for building success: Standing out from the crowd. Remember back in the mid 2000's when everyone and their brother started saying you need to blog? Well guess what, it looks like everyone and their sister listened and then some. Best estimates on how many blogs are out there put the number at close to 250 million active blogs.

If you compare that to podcasting, iTunes says there are 250,000 podcasts in iTunes. With only about half of those being active (updated in the last three months), that gives you a blogger to podcaster ratio of roughly 2,000 to 1. If you have a blog covering a specific subject, typically there will be 2,000 bloggers to each podcaster covering that subject. Having a blog no longer separates you from the crowd – blogging is the crowd. If you want to step away from and above your peers – having a podcast is the perfect way to do that. I just want to state that ratio again – 2,000 bloggers for each podcaster – 2,000:1. Put another way... if you filled the Madison Square Garden up with bloggers, only 10 people in the building would be podcasters, and my guess is they likely would be the ones on the court.

If you are a female blogger – the ratio is much worse or better depending on your perspective. Only 13% of all podcasters are female vs 52% of bloggers being female. That means there is a 7,800 to 1 ratio of female bloggers to female podcasters. If you are a women and blogging, then podcasting is a way for you to quickly stand out from your peers.

This difference in these ratios is why, as a podcaster, you are looked at with a more authoritative view vs. a blogger who is looked at as really just another face in the crowd.

Today is the day for you to start podcasting.

– Rob Walch (Podcaster since 2004)
VP of Podcaster Relations at Libsyn.com
Host of *podCast411* and *Today in iOS*
Co-Author of *Tricks of the Podcasting Masters*

Made in the USA
Middletown, DE
11 September 2017